The S-1___

A COACHING HANDBOOK

essential principles and practical ideas
for coaching in the workplace

Alison Haill

Published by Oxford Professional Consulting Ltd
Prama House, 267 Banbury Road, Summertown, Oxford, OX2 7HT

First published 2008

ISBN 978-0-9560233-0-8

Acknowledgements
The author would like to thank Jackie Arnold for her support and ideas during the coach training programmes of 2006-8 which they delivered together and which provided the catalyst for this book. Acknowledgements are also due to Sir John Whitmore for the GROW model, The Coaching Academy for their Wheel of Life which contributed to the creation of the S-Factor and Paul Avins for the Above The Line concept.

About the author

Alison Haill is an accomplished trainer as well as an executive and corporate coach. She has a strong track record working with leaders at all levels across sectors, from engineering to education, the oil industry to advertising. As a motivational trainer for over 20 years, and an inspiring coach for corporate clients and organisations of all sizes in the UK and overseas, she works with leaders and teams to improve performance, communication and results. She is Managing Director of the training and coaching consultancy Oxford Professional Consulting, which she founded in Oxford in 1998. She is a member of the Society for Intercultural Education Training and Research, the UK Association for Coaching and the International Coaching Federation. She has two Masters degrees, a PGCE and several coaching qualifications.

Oxford Professional Consulting has recently been invited to work with UK local authorities and schools to introduce coaching into education management. So, alongside her core work with businesses, Alison works as a coach for headteachers, delivers coaching skills workshops for leaders, managers and staff at all levels in education, and is training a team of education coaches to work with UK schools.

CONTENTS

List of worksheets, coaching tools, models, phrases and records

Chapter 1	Introduction	1
Chapter 2	The S-Factor	9
Chapter 3	Working with wheels	17
Chapter 4	S-Wheels	35
Chapter 5	Key coaching principles	51
Chapter 6	Key coaching skills	57
Chapter 7	Remarkable progress	67
Chapter 8	Celebration	77
Chapter 9	Limiting language	85
Chapter 10	Documentation, contracts and agreements	95
Chapter 11	Coaching in Management	105
Chapter 12	Coaching in Education	113
Chapter 13	Continuing Professional Development	121
Chapter 14	Three favourites	129
Chapter 15	Your own records	139

Checklist of coaching tools

1. S-GROW model   10
2. Wheels - labelled   20
3. S-Wheels - labelled   36
4. Blank wheels   30, 46
5. ERR model   72
6. SPOT diagram   70
7. Deep listening / listening at Level 3   57
8. Questions, questioning skills   58
9. S-Questions   11
10. Reflecting back phrases   60
11. Challenging   59
12. Clarifying / checking understanding   61
13. Summarising + phrases   61
14. Parking issues   62
15. Positive language   87
16. Half-full or half-empty   86
17. Positive self-talk (affirmations)   87
18. Goal Setting   67
19. Goal Record Sheet   80
20. Coaching Record Sheet   97
21. Individual Planner Sheet with sample   98
22. Coaching Agreement   101
23. Coaching Preparation Form   100
24. Getting Present exercise   129
25. Above The Line   130
26. Evaluating My Coaching Skills - checklist   141
27. Fact and Fiction   132
28. Gaining commitment through scaling 0-10   90

List of photocopiable worksheets included

charts, diagrams, templates and models

		pages
1.	Job Performance Wheel	20
2.	Management Wheel	22
3.	Teaching Wheel	24
4.	Personal Wheel	26
5.	Admin Wheel	28
6.	Evaluation Wheel – blank	30
7.	Job Performance S-Wheel	36
8.	Management S-Wheel	38
9.	Teaching S-Wheel	40
10.	Personal S-Wheel	42
11.	Admin S-Wheel	44
12.	Evaluation S-Wheel – blank	46
13.	Action Plan	79
14.	SPOT diagram	70
15.	Glass Half-full	86
16.	Goal Record Sheet	80
17.	Coaching Record Sheet	97
18.	Individual Planner Sheet	98
19.	Individual Preparation Form	100
20.	Coaching Agreement	101
21.	Above the Line	131
22.	Fact & Fiction	133
23.	Evaluating My Coaching Skills	141
24.	Coaching Hours	142
25.	CPD Records and Notes	143

Coaching models included

S-GROW

ERR

Questions and phrases

S-Questions

Questions

Reflecting-back phrases

SMART Goals

First Step questions

Extra S-Questions

Your own records - photocopiable

Coaching Ideas to Try

Coaching Hours

CPD records

Useful Contacts and Phone Numbers

Chapter 1

Introduction

What is the S-Factor? What is coaching? To start with the second question, confusion and a profusion of meanings for *coaching* abound today. Coaching is used to describe one-on-one lessons for a student, a remedial process for underperforming employees, and for the mix of motivation, training and polishing given by the sports coach to high-level sports champions and by the voice coach to world-class opera singers.

The focus of this book is coaching in the workplace, as a key leadership and development skill to benefit individuals at every level in an organisation. This book defines coaching as:

> **structured conversation and a rigorous process which brings results; its aim is to develop an individual or individuals both professionally and personally, optimising their potential in work and life, maximising performance and acting as a catalyst to creative thinking, new opportunities and inspiring results.**

To clarify further, coaching is not telling, advising or counselling, neither is it mentoring. In differentiating between mentoring and coaching we follow the International Coaching Federation and the Institute of Leadership and Management (ILM). While both coaching and mentoring centre on the coachee and their desired outcomes, the mentor usually gives advice whereas coaches use incisive questioning to help coachees think through and produce their own solutions.

The benefits of coaching are many: in attitude, motivation, responsibility, teamwork. Coaching heightens awareness of communication and language, personal and professional strengths, as well as areas to develop, opportunities and potential. It creates and builds confidence, creative-thinking, responsibility and commitment. It allows time to reflect, so develops thinking skills, planning and therefore results.

Who is this book for?

While our own work is with leaders in companies and organisations, this handbook is written for all who coach in the workplace, as well as for any professionals interested in using coaching as a development process with others or for themselves. Whether you are new to the skills of coaching or experienced, we believe that the reminders collected here will be useful.

Developing coaching skills

Used in your coaching practice, this handbook will help in planning and delivery. Not only will it give you ideas when you are planning your sessions but by being spiral-bound it will stay open at the page you need, to act as a discreet reminder during the coaching session itself.

As a coach, you will find it a source of key principles and tips. In addition, it is important to continue to grow and develop your skills, building up ideas in an organised way so that they are at your fingertips when needed. After a coaching conversation you will often reflect on something you might do differently next time – or have a brainwave for your coaching in general - but by the next session it has gone. Capture those thoughts in the Own Notes pages, using this book to build up your own list of coaching tips and ideas.

Professional development for managers and leaders

Coaching skills may already be part of your managing or leadership style. If so, refresh your thinking or find new ideas in this book. If not, give them a try to complement what you already do or to use alone in specific one-on-one contexts, such as performance management interviews or appraisal meetings, as well as with teams.

Self-development

Many coaching ideas can be used for self-development if you do not want to work with a coach, or alongside the work you do with your coach. However, if you currently prefer working alone on personal and professional development, do consider the additional dimension that a coach could give you. The dialogue with a coach produces different insights to those that come when you work alone.

Tips on using this book

Take 10 minutes to skim through the whole book. Look through the book and mark pages that catch your attention. Write these in the Coaching Ideas To Try page at the back of the book, adding to this list as ideas occur later.

Use the diagrams in the book to print handouts for coachees. The diagrams and models in the book are all photocopiable but remember to enlarge to A4 for easier use. The diagrams are also available in CD Rom form so that you can print out your own.

Have the book with you whenever you coach. In a coaching session, you may want to glance at a page or use the prompts to help you formulate questions or other phrases. You may look up a model or tool that you did not bring with you. If so, showing the diagram in the book to your client or coachee may be enough to prompt their thoughts so that they can jot their own notes on paper; or they may copy the layout from your page. If a copier or scanner is available, make a copy on the spot.

Use the book when planning a coaching session. Remind yourself of the key principles of coaching; look up useful questions and comments you might use; re-read the early S-Chapters so that you keep the S-Factor in mind. When you are a new coach, it is helpful to keep the S-GROW page open beside you.

Use the Own Notes pages at the end of each chapter. Catch the moment: if something occurs to you when reviewing a session, note it down in the Own Notes, near to the skills or tool it applies to. A good coach spends some minutes after each coaching session to reflect on the coachee's learnings and their own - how it went, what went well, what they might do differently next time. At this point, you may have a great idea for the future so write it in this book. There are pages after each chapter and at the back.

Fill in the Coaching CPD page. This will remind you to keep building your coaching skills. What you learn from being coached, from other coaching professionals, further courses and reading, will complement your practical coaching experience and help you coach more effectively and professionally. Again, keeping a record of these CPD items acknowledges your achievements as well as motivating you to keep developing your skills.

Keep a running total on the Coaching Hours page. As you grow in experience, it is important to keep a tally of the number of hours of coaching you have done.

Obviously practising coaching will eventually make you an experienced coach but keep a running total of your practical coaching hours for two other good reasons.

First, totting up the hours gives you a sense of your own progress. Secondly, as the coaching profession matures, it is no longer enough to say you are a coach. Increasingly, employers are asking searching questions of those who say they coach. You may be asked what coaching qualifications you hold, what was included in the course, how many coaching hours you have done, what models you use, what ethics you sign up to, which professional coaching associations you are member of, and more.

This approach is to be welcomed, because it shows your experience and professionalism is valued. If you are serious about being a good professional coach, this will spur you on.

In the Total Hours, include any *buddy coaching* you do, any coaching sessions for friends as well as time spent coaching in work. Also add in the hours of practical coaching completed for any coaching qualifications. Write your current total now, with today's date, in the space in Chapter 13.

Keep up your coaching practice. You will hone your skills if you use them often, so give yourself a goal of how many hours to complete by when. Write that down with today's date and the specific date you want to achieve it by. Be sure to update your running total with actual competion dates – weekly, monthly or whatever suits your worklife.

Use the write-in pages. When you make your own notes in this handbook you will always have everything together. Flicking through it before a session, your eye will fall on one of your own creative ideas jotted down earlier – it may be just the one you need. The book is designed with double pages for handwritten notes after every chapter; your notes are separated from printed pages of text - to please those users who find handwriting in a printed book unappealing!

Client, coachee or learner?

This book uses *coach* for the person employing coaching skills while *coachee* and *client* are used interchangeably for the person being coached. In a sense the individual being coached at work is a client even if they are a colleague: the coach should treat them with the same respect as if they were paying and give them excellent value. The term *learner* would be equally valid because each person being coached is a learner, whether learning to be more aware of poor work-life balance and how to address it or how to restructure their company and give better share-holder value.

Own Notes

Own Notes

Chapter 2

The S-Factor

What is the S-Factor?

The S of S-Factor stands for Successes and Strengths. Coaching which takes time to acknowledge successes and strengths as well as problems tends to enable coachees to think more creatively: they start from a more confident and happier place where creativity flourishes more naturally.

To this end, we introduce the S-Factor into several conventional coaching activities: the S-Wheel, the S-GROW and the use of S-Questions. The result is that coach and coachee alike develop the habit of noticing success and strength areas rather than focusing immediately on areas to develop and on problems to solve. There will always be the latter at work and in life, whether we call them challenges or issues, but this way more and better solutions are found – and more easily.

The GROW and S-GROW models

The GROW model is often one of the first coaching ideas that a learner coach meets. Created by Sir John Whitmore, it is a model for achieving goals, deciding dilemmas and solving problems.

The power of the GROW model is that it is very easy to understand and to apply, while at the same time being very thorough. Once understood, it is applicable and effective for a multitude of contexts, situations and concerns.

It even enables individuals to make progress on complex problems or issues where they have felt 'stuck' for a long time.

The GROW model consists of these four steps:

G   Goal Where you are going, what you want to achieve

R   Reality Where you are now vis à vis the goal

O   Opportunities Options available to reach this goal

W   Will What you will do to make it happen

GROW works very well but S-GROW is even more effective. What I have discovered with my colleagues and clients is that an initial step before GROW makes the whole process more successful: this is how the S-Factor was born.

By including the Success and Strength factor, we create a more powerful process. Our preferred model is therefore the S-GROW.

The S-GROW model

S   Successes and strengths In the job, at home

G   Goal Where you are going, what you want to achieve

R   Reality Where you are now vis à vis the goal

O   Opportunities Options available to reach this goal

W   Will What you will do to make it happen

By starting with successes, the S-GROW process begins on a happier note and, more importantly, two further benefits are achieved:

1. The clients remember their recent successes
2. As a result they think more creatively in the session.

The first of these is enormously important. As a rule we tend to enjoy our successes fleetingly and many of them we do not even recognise as successes. Often a client will at first have difficulty in finding any successes at all in their past week. They have come to the session ready to talk about things that are NOT working. Getting into the habit of acknowledging and celebrating success is a way to increase our power to think creatively, be productive and happy. So working with your coachees to inculcate this habit is a very positive step towards helping them to use more of their latent potential.

Many coachees, however successful they may seem to be, lack confidence in some area. S-Factor coaching helps their confidence to grow healthily, by encouraging them to savour success in a different way. Starting the coaching with an S-Question is an easy way to create a more positive frame of mind. You will find that your coachee values the S-Factor, so do not be tempted to 'save time' by missing it out.

If it is not convenient at the start of the session or if you forget, you can ask an S-Question later on. For instance with S-GROW, the S-Factor might come after the Goal phase.

Getting to S

You can start the coaching conversation with an S-Question such as those below.

Note that one strength or success is not enough. I normally try to get two or three. It is beneficial to keep that positive feeling a little longer than just 20 seconds.

Also, you are building a habit here, of finding and focusing on the positives not just the negatives in work and life. Keep a close watch on the client's face and you will see how it lightens up as, say, they remember that their daughter was accepted for university this week or they had good feedback from a new idea at work.

S-Questions

Try one of these S-Questions

- *What has gone well this week?*
- *What's going well in your work at the moment?*
- *What successes have you had this week?*

- *What do you enjoy at work at the moment?*
- *And what is good at home?*
- *....... in the family?*
- *....... with your golf / squash / at the gym?*
- *What are your strengths as a leader (manager, teacher, parent)?*

Use supplementary questions, as shown above, if the client has trouble finding successes or strengths.

Other useful prompts are:

- *What might your colleagues say your strengths are?*
- *What might your mother / father / child / secretary say?*
- *What would your best friend or your worst enemy say?*

Own Notes

Own Notes

Chapter 3

Working with Wheels

A simple and effective tool for coaches is the Evaluation Wheel.

Probably the reason for the popularity of the wheel shape in coaching is due to its clear visual impact but, added to that, it is a concept of great simplicity, quick and easy to complete with an effective result. An Evaluation Wheel takes only minutes to complete but that time can involve deep thought and evaluative processes. The result is often surprising in what it reveals: the balance of success and struggle is often more positive than expected and the way forward surprisingly clear.

The Evaluation Wheel can be used for a quick overview in many situations, such as:

- Considering job performance
- Choosing a focus
- Analysing a problem
- Evaluating achievements
- Assessing progress in a to-do list
- Decision-making
- Professional development
- Coaching

In coaching, the Evaluation Wheel gives the coachee an easy unthreatening route to describing the totality of work, or a decision, problem or project. It provides a focus for the coach and coachee, allowing both to receive a great deal of information in a structured way, without the need for numerous questions.

The wheel also helps the coachee to see the strengths and areas for development in any given situation. Those who tend to denigrate their own success can be guided by the coach to acknowedge achievements. While for those who easily notice their successes but have difficulty in seeing how to optimise their potential, the wheel provides the coach with a springboard for probing questions which help the coachee to uncover a new way forward.

Using the diagrams

The diagrams following are ready for copying and enlarging to A4 size; a CD Rom of printable documents is also available.

Each diagram contains 8 labels relevant to the context indicated. For example, our Job Performance Wheel indicates 8 specific areas involved in job performance. Of course this is not the only way that this topic could be broken up.

The diagrams included here do work well. However, if your client wishes to cross out and change some categories, that is also fine – and can be done during the session. If you prefer to design your own headings, use the blank Evaluation Wheel which is included at the end of this chapter. We suggest working with a pencil rather than ink since clients often want to change their minds.

Some coaches like to have the client complete the wheel in the meeting or coaching session, while others give it as a task to do at home.

A Job Performance Wheel

Today's date....................

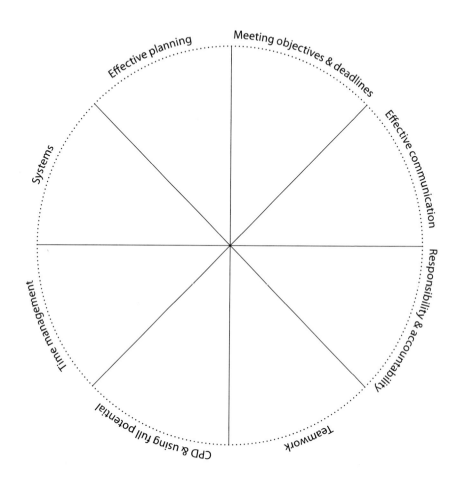

Effective planning

Meeting objectives & deadlines

Effective communication

Systems

Responsibility & accountability

Time management

Teamwork

CPD & using full potential

Notes on using a Job Performance Wheel

1. Tell your coachee:
   The circle is divided into sections to reflect 8 parts of your job. If you want to re-word a label, please do.

   This is a useful tool to quickly assess how your job performance is going at present.

2. Ask your coachee to shade in each segment according to how satisfied they are with how that area is going, with 0 (zero satisfaction) at the centre of the circle and 10 (fully satisfied) at the rim.

3. When the 8 sections are complete, have the client add the day's date. Then you start a conversation, perhaps with one or more of these:
   How did you find that task?
   What did you discover in completing the Wheel?
   So, talk me through your Wheel. Start where you like.

4. The coach needs to manage the time. If the coachee gets stuck on one segment, you may prompt them to go round the whole circle before choosing one area to focus on in more detail. Or you may straightaway let the coachee choose a segment to focus on:
   And the next segment?
   Take me round the whole circle to get the full picture.
   Choose which segment you'd like to work on today.

Reminders

- Always date the Wheel so you can refer back
- Let the client decide the focus and change labels if need be
- Key question to move forward in an area or task:
  What one step could you take to improve the situation?

A Management Wheel

Today's date.....................

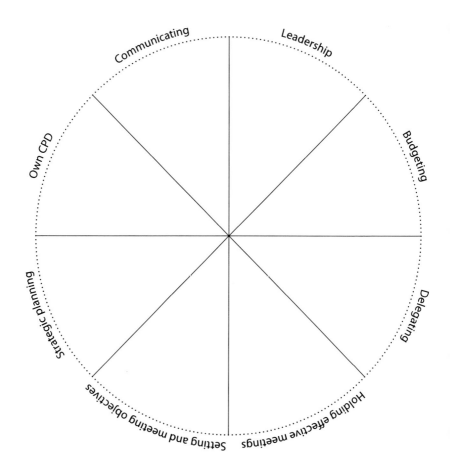

Notes on using a Management Wheel

1. Tell your coachee:
   The circle is divided into sections to reflect 8 parts of your managerial role. If you want to re-word it, do.

   This is a useful tool to quickly assess how you see your management skills at present.

2. Ask your coachee to shade in each segment according to how satisfied they are with how that area is going, with 0 (zero satisfaction) at the centre of the circle and 10 (fully satisfied) at the rim.

3. When the 8 sections are complete, have the client add the day's date. Then you start a conversation, perhaps with one or more of these:
   How did you find that task?
   What did you discover in completing the Wheel?
   So, talk me through your Wheel. Start where you like.

4. The coach needs to manage the time. If the coachee gets stuck on one segment, you may prompt them to go round the whole circle before choosing one area to focus on in more detail. Or you may straightaway let the coachee choose a segment to focus on:
   And the next segment?
   Take me round the whole circle to get the full picture.
   Choose which segment you'd like to work on today.

Reminders

- Always date the Wheel so you can refer back
- Let the client decide the focus and change labels if need be
- Key question to move forward in an area or task:
  What one step could you take to improve the situation?

A Teaching Wheel

Today's date.....................

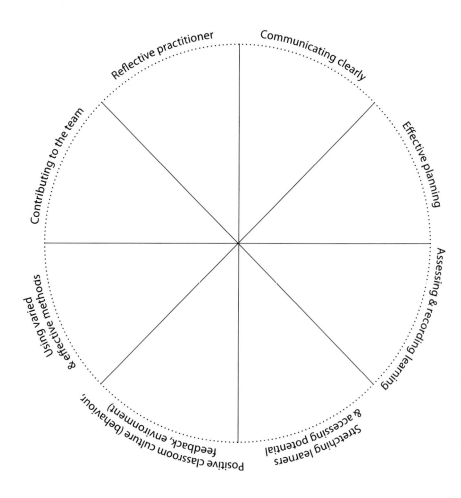

Notes on using a Teaching Wheel

1. Tell your coachee:
   The circle is divided into sections to reflect 8 parts of your teaching role. If you want to re-word a label, do.

   This is a useful tool to quickly assess how you see your teaching role at present.

2. Ask your coachee to shade in each segment according to how satisfied they are with how that area is going, with 0 (zero satisfaction) at the centre of the circle and 10 (fully satisfied) at the rim.

3. When the 8 sections are complete, have the client add the day's date. Then you start a conversation, perhaps with one or more of these:
   How did you find that task?
   What did you discover in completing the Wheel?
   So, talk me through your Wheel. Start where you like.

4. The coach needs to manage the time. If the coachee gets stuck on one segment, you may prompt them to go round the whole circle before choosing one area to focus on in more detail. Or you may straightaway let the coachee choose a segment to focus on:
   And the next segment?
   Take me round the whole circle to get the full picture.
   Choose which segment you'd like to work on today.

Reminders

- Always date the Wheel so you can refer back
- Let the client decide the focus and change labels if need be
- Key question to move forward in an area or task:
  What one step could you take to improve the situation?

A Personal Wheel

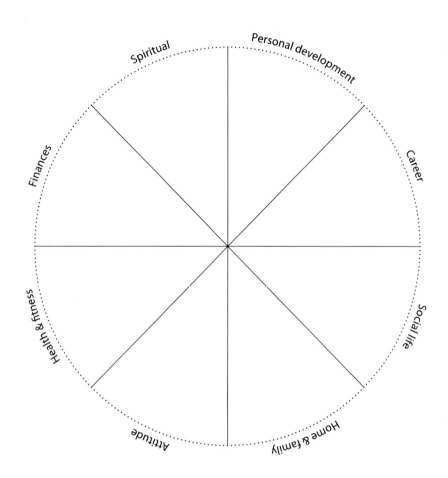

Notes on using a Personal Wheel

1. Tell your coachee:
   The circle is divided into sections to reflect 8 parts of your life. If you want to re-word a label, do.

   This is a useful tool to quickly assess how you see your life at present.

2. Ask your coachee to shade in each segment according to how satisfied they are with how that area is going, with 0 (zero satisfaction) at the centre of the circle and 10 (fully satisfied) at the rim.

3. When the 8 sections are complete, have the client add the day's date. Then you start a conversation, perhaps with one or more of these:
   How did you find that task?
   What did you discover in completing the Wheel?
   So, talk me through your Wheel. Start where you like.

4. The coach needs to manage the time. If the coachee gets stuck on one segment, you may prompt them to go round the whole circle before choosing one area to focus on in more detail. Or you may straightaway let the coachee choose a segment to focus on:
   And the next segment?
   Take me round the whole circle to get the full picture.
   Choose which segment you'd like to work on today.

Reminders

- Always date the Wheel so you can refer back
- Let the client decide the focus and change labels if need be
- Key question to move forward in an area or task:
  What one step could you take to improve the situation?

An Admin Wheel

Today's date....................

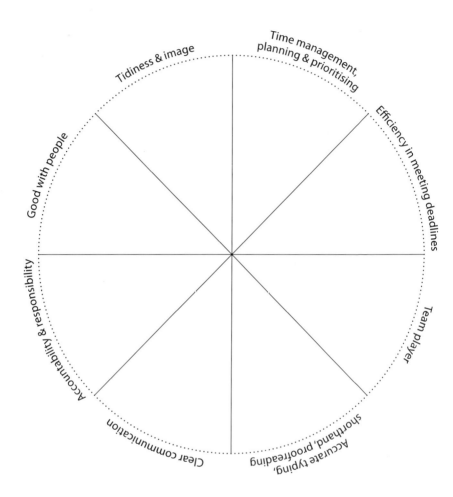

Time management, planning & prioritising

Efficiency in meeting deadlines

Team player

Accurate typing, shorthand, proofreading

Clear communication

Accountability & responsibility

Good with people

Tidiness & image

Notes on using an Admin Wheel

1. Tell your coachee:
   The circle is divided into sections to reflect 8 parts of your admin role. If you want to re-word the labels, do.

   This is a useful tool to quickly assess how you see your job at present.

2. Ask your coachee to shade in each segment according to how satisfied they are with how that area is going, with 0 (zero satisfaction) at the centre of the circle and 10 (fully satisfied) at the rim.

3. When the 8 sections are complete, have the client add the day's date. Then you start a conversation, perhaps with one or more of these:
   How did you find that task?
   What did you discover in completing the Wheel?
   So, talk me through your Wheel. Start where you like.

4. The coach needs to manage the time. If the coachee gets stuck on one segment, you may prompt them to go round the whole circle before choosing one area to focus on in more detail. Or you may straightaway let the coachee choose a segment to focus on:
   And the next segment?
   Take me round the whole circle to get the full picture.
   Choose which segment you'd like to work on today.

Reminders

- Always date the Wheel so you can refer back
- Let the client decide the focus and change labels if need be
- Key question to move forward in an area or task:
  What one step could you take to improve the situation?

The Evaluation Wheel

Today's date....................

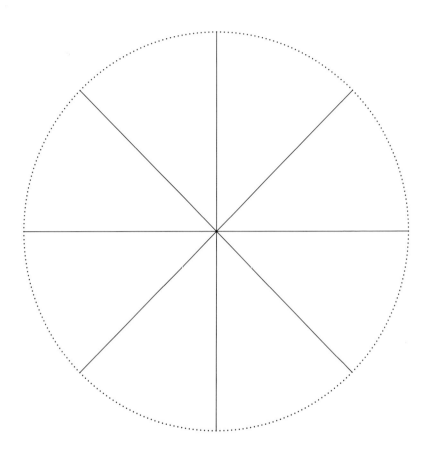

Notes on using the Evaluation Wheel

1. Tell your coachee:
   The circle is divided into sections to reflect 8 parts of a project, job, issue. Choose a label for each segment.

   This is a useful tool to quickly evaluate the current situation as regards that project, job, issue.

2. Ask your coachee to shade in each segment according to how satisfied they are with how that area is going, with 0 (zero satisfaction) at the centre of the circle and 10 (fully satisfied) at the rim.

3. When the 8 sections are complete, have the client add the day's date. Then you start a conversation, perhaps with one or more of these:
   How did you find that task?
   What did you discover in completing the Wheel?
   So, talk me through your Wheel. Start where you like.

4. The coach needs to manage the time. If the coachee gets stuck on one segment, you may prompt them to go round the whole circle before choosing one area to focus on in more detail. Or you may straightaway let the coachee choose a segment to focus on:
   And the next segment?
   Take me round the whole circle to get the full picture.
   Choose which segment you'd like to work on today.

Reminders

- Always date the Wheel so you can refer back
- Let the client decide the focus and change labels if need be
- Key question to move forward in an area or task:
  What one step could you take to improve the situation?

Own Notes

Own Notes

Chapter 4

S-Wheels

The S-Wheel adds an important S-Factor element to the Evaluation Wheel: the Success and Strengths factor.

For each segment the coachee notes down a bullet point list of related Strengths. For example, if a segment of the Wheel is labelled Delegation Skills, the corresponding S-Box might be:

> - **am delegating to X already**
> - **boss Y is a good model**
> - **delegating already at home**
> - **delegated Task A in May**

The coach might prompt this activity with questions, such as:

What have you delegated already?
Who do you know who delegates well?
Which of your team would welcome some of your tasks?
What could you read to give you ideas on delegating?

By filling in the S-Box, the client soon finds that they have strengths, a track record and available options related to this field which they may not have been aware of.

The S-Box is filled in **after** doing the wheel activity in the normal way already described. Or you can have the coachee fill in the S-Boxes first. Note the differences when you change the order of events! Whichever you choose, using the S-Box will raise the coachee's expectations of success, which in turn encourages them to take action. The S-Wheel therefore works as both an evaluation or planning tool and an encouragement to action.

The Job Performance S-Wheel

Strengths

Strengths

Strengths

Strengths

Strengths

Strengths

Strengths

Strengths

Effective communication

Responsibility & accountability

Meeting objectives & deadlines

Teamwork

Effective planning

CPD & using full potential

Systems

Time management

Notes on using a Job Performance S-Wheel

Important

If you have never used a Wheel in coaching before, work with one of the Evaluation Wheels in Chapter 3 before using an S-Wheel. So that when you start on this page, you will be confident about using Wheels and will not have to flip back and forwards between pages.

1. Have your coachee complete the Wheel as in Chapter 3.

2. Explain how to use the S-Boxes:
   Each segment has an S-Box attached in which you list your Strengths in this area. Include relevant Skills you already have; relevant Successes you have had; Sources of information such as people or experts you could ask; models or people you could copy.

3. If needed, prompt your coachee with these questions:
   What strengths do you have in this area already?
   What skills do you have which could help you here?
   Who do you know who could be helpful here?

4. When all the S-Boxes are complete, start a conversation, eg:
   How did you find this model / exercise?
   What did you discover in filling in the S-Boxes?
   Where would you like to focus now?

Reminders

- Ensure the client dates the Wheel each time so you can refer back
- Consider each S-Box. The benefit for the coachee is to rediscover strengths to build on and potential "allies".
- The coach needs to manage the time
- Let the client decide the segment to focus on first
- Key questions:
  What could you do to improve the situation?
  What one step could you take to improve the situation?

The Management S-Wheel

Strengths

Strengths

Strengths

Strengths

Strengths

Strengths

Strengths

Strengths

Budgeting

Delegating

Holding effective meetings

Setting and meeting objectives

Strategic planning

Own CPD

Communicating

Leadership

Notes on using a Management S-Wheel

Important

If you have never used a Wheel in coaching before, work with one of the Evaluation Wheels in Chapter 3 before using an S-Wheel. So that when you start on this page, you will be confident about using Wheels and will not have to flip back and forwards between pages.

1. Have your coachee complete the Wheel as in Chapter 3.

2. Explain how to use the S-Boxes:
   Each segment has an S-Box attached in which you list your Strengths in this area. Include relevant Skills you already have; relevant Successes you have had; Sources of information such as people or experts you could ask, models you could copy.

3. If needed, prompt your coachee with these questions:
   What strengths do you have in this area already?
   What skills do you have which could help you here?
   Who do you know who could be helpful here?

4. When all the S-Boxes are complete, start a conversation, eg:
   How did you find this model / exercise?
   What did you discover in filling in the S-Boxes?
   Where would you like to focus now?

Reminders

- Ensure the client dates the Wheel each time so you can refer back
- Consider each S-Box. The benefit for the coachee is to rediscover strengths to build on and potential "allies".
- The coach needs to manage the time
- Let the client decide the segment to focus on first
- Key questions:
  What could you do to improve the situation?
  What one step could you take to improve the situation?

The Teaching S-Wheel

Strengths

Strengths

Strengths

Strengths

Strengths

Strengths

Strengths

Strengths

Effective planning

Assessing & recording learning

Stretching & accessing potential

feedback, environment (behaviour, culture)

Communicating clearly

Reflective practitioner

Contributing to the team

Using varied & effective methods

Notes on using a Teaching S-Wheel

Important

If you have never used a Wheel in coaching before, work with one of the
Evaluation Wheels in Chapter 3 before using an S-Wheel. So that when
you start on this page, you will be confident about using Wheels and will
not have to flip back and forwards between pages.

1. Have your coachee complete the Wheel as in Chapter 3.

2. Explain how to use the S-Boxes:
   *Each segment has an S-Box attached in which you list your
   Strengths in this area. Include relevant Skills you already have;
   relevant Successes you have had; Sources of information such
   as people or experts you could ask, models you could copy.*

3. If needed, prompt your coachee with these questions:
   What strengths do you have in this area already?
   What skills do you have which could help you here?
   Who do you know who could be helpful here?

4. When all the S-Boxes are complete, start a
   conversation, eg:
   How did you find this model / exercise?
   What did you discover in filling in the S-Boxes?
   Where would you like to focus now?

Reminders

- Ensure the client dates the Wheel each time so you
  can refer back
- Consider each S-Box. The benefit for the coachee is to
  rediscover strengths to build on and potential "allies".
- The coach needs to manage the time
- Let the client decide the segment to focus on first
- Key questions:
  What could you do to improve the situation?
  What one step could you take to improve the situation?

The Personal S-Wheel

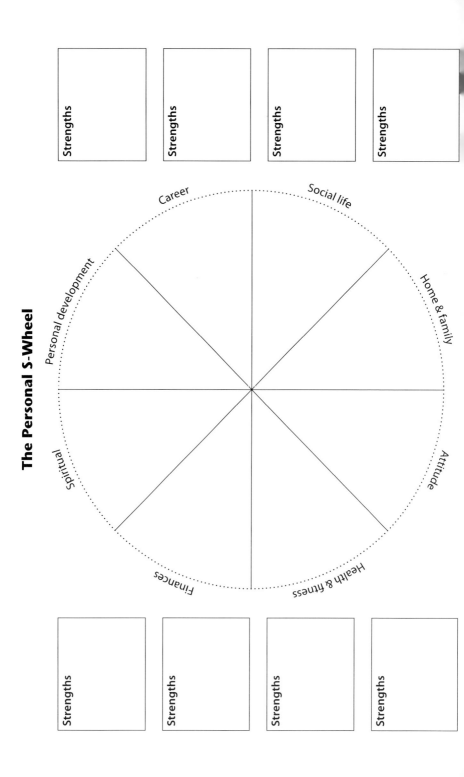

Strengths

Strengths

Strengths

Strengths

Strengths

Strengths

Strengths

Strengths

Career

Social life

Personal development

Home & family

Spiritual

Attitude

Finances

Health & fitness

Notes on using a Personal S-Wheel

Important

If you have never used a Wheel in coaching before, work with one of the Evaluation Wheels in Chapter 3 before using an S-Wheel. So that when you start on this page, you will be confident about using Wheels and will not have to flip back and forwards between pages.

1. Have your coachee complete the Wheel as in Chapter 3.

2. Explain how to use the S-Boxes:
   Each segment has an S-Box attached in which you list your Strengths in this area. Include relevant Skills you already have; relevant Successes you have had; Sources of information such as people or experts you could ask, models you could copy.

3. If needed, prompt your coachee with these questions:
   What strengths do you have in this area already?
   What skills do you have which could help you here?
   Who do you know who could be helpful here?

4. When all the S-Boxes are complete, start a conversation, eg:
   How did you find this model / exercise?
   What did you discover in filling in the S-Boxes?
   Where would you like to focus now?

Reminders

- Ensure the client dates the Wheel each time so you can refer back
- Consider each S-Box. The benefit for the coachee is to rediscover strengths to build on and potential "allies".
- The coach needs to manage the time
- Let the client decide the segment to focus on first
- Key questions:
  What could you do to improve the situation?
  What one step could you take to improve the situation?

The Admin S-Wheel

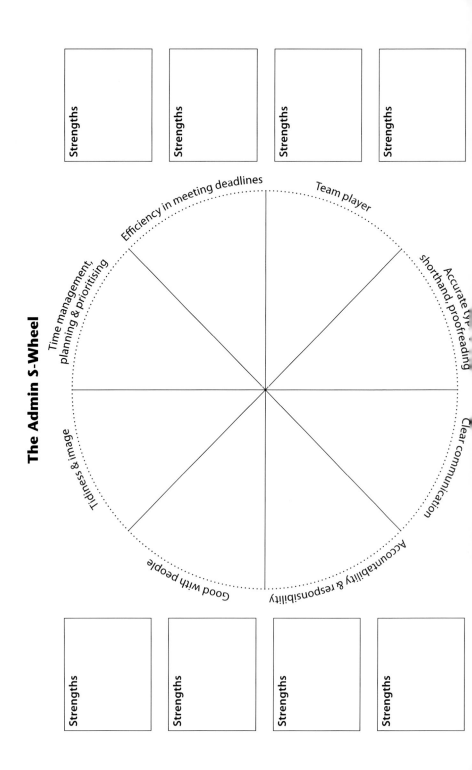

Strengths (×4, top)

Strengths (×4, bottom)

Efficiency in meeting deadlines

Team player

Time management, planning & prioritising

Accurate typing, shorthand, proofreading

Tidiness & image

Clear communication

Good with people

Accountability & responsibility

Notes on using an Admin S-Wheel

Important

If you have never used a Wheel in coaching before, work with one of the Evaluation Wheels in Chapter 3 before using an S-Wheel. So that when you start on this page, you will be confident about using Wheels and will not have to flip back and forwards between pages.

1. Have your coachee complete the Wheel as in Chapter 3.

2. Explain how to use the S-Boxes:
   Each segment has an S-Box attached in which you list your Strengths in this area. Include relevant Skills you already have; relevant Successes you have had; Sources of information such as people or experts you could ask, models you could copy.

3. If needed, prompt your coachee with these questions:
   What strengths do you have in this area already?
   What skills do you have which could help you here?
   Who do you know who could be helpful here?

4. When all the S-Boxes are complete, start a conversation, eg:
   How did you find this model / exercise?
   What did you discover in filling in the S-Boxes?
   Where would you like to focus now?

Reminders

- Ensure the client dates the Wheel each time so you can refer back
- Consider each S-Box. The benefit for the coachee is to rediscover strengths to build on and potential "allies".
- The coach needs to manage the time
- Let the client decide the segment to focus on first
- Key questions:
  What could you do to improve the situation?
  What one step could you take to improve the situation?

The Evaluation S-Wheel

Strengths

Strengths

Strengths

Strengths

Strengths

Strengths

Strengths

Strengths

Notes on using the Evaluation S-Wheel

Important

If you have never used a Wheel in coaching before, work with one of the Evaluation Wheels in Chapter 3 before using an S-Wheel. So that when you start on this page, you will be confident about using Wheels and will not have to flip back and forwards between pages.

1. Have your coachee complete the Wheel as in Chapter 3.

2. Explain how to use the S-Boxes:
   Each segment has an S-Box attached in which you list your Strengths in this area. Include relevant Skills you already have; relevant Successes you have had; Sources of information such as people or experts you could ask, models you could copy.

3. If needed, prompt your coachee with these questions:
   What strengths do you have in this area already?
   What skills do you have which could help you here?
   Who do you know who could be helpful here?

4. When all the S-Boxes are complete, start a conversation, eg:
   How did you find this model / exercise?
   What did you discover in filling in the S-Boxes?
   Where would you like to focus now?

Reminders

- Ensure the client dates the Wheel each time so you can refer back
- Consider each S-Box. The benefit for the coachee is to rediscover strengths to build on and potential "allies".
- The coach needs to manage the time
- Let the client decide the segment to focus on first
- Key questions:
  What could you do to improve the situation?
  What one step could you take to improve the situation?

Own Notes

Own Notes

Chapter 5

Key Coaching Principles

The coachee chooses the goal

Coaching is about progress, creative thinking and maximising the potential of the client. Fundamental to this, and what makes it successful, is that the **coachee** chooses the goal in the coaching conversation. In this way the coachee is motivated to take action. On the other hand, if the goal is imposed, it is very likely that the coachee will agree actions but not carry them out.

Where coaching is initiated as a result of a need to raise performance or due to poor performance, this rule is still relevant. Say the coaching is set up for Jim because of poor performance and the boss wants Jim to meet deadlines reliably. Within those parameters, the coach needs to ensure Jim finds an outcome that motivates him. After some questioning from the coach, Jim decides what he would really like is to meet all deadlines easily and learn strategies to manage time better so he can enjoy free weekends with his family. This is now Jim's goal and he is motivated to reach it.

Once Jim has found and articulated his goal, the coach's job is to support him in reaching it through the coaching process.

Believing in the coachee's potential

One cornerstone of coaching, rather than of mentoring or teaching, is that the coach believes that the coachee has the answers or has the potential to find them. The coaching process does not work so effectively if coaches believe they must give the answers, because then the clients **expect** to be given answers: thus they avoid exercising their own creative thinking and keep the lid on their own potential.

For many coaches this is hard. Some of us are so used to evaluating others that we do it unconsciously. Witness the terms we hear, even if we do not always label others aloud like this: *high-potentials, high-fliers, successful, wonderful, go-getters, no-hopers, hopeless, weak performers.* From business to education, colleagues judge each other at work as regards productivity, attractiveness, success at work, sociability and in many other areas. Those whose job role includes assessing performance (such as managers, Human Resource professionals, teachers) often find it hardest to avoid evaluating and judging others when coaching.

So the coach needs to prepare for coaching, clearing the mind of its normal judging and evaluating activities, creating a mindset of total belief in the client and the client's potential.

Being *unattached to the outcome*

Closely linked to this is the need for the coach to remain *unattached to the outcome* of the coaching. When we are *attached* to it, we skew the conversation so that the coachee comes out with our answer and not their own. When we want their success too much, we tend to put too much of ourselves and our own creative thinking into the conversation, providing the client with answers. Not only does this prevent the client from learning to think differently and from the sense of achievement in finding their own solutions, but our answers suit *us* and may not suit *them*.

The coach needs to learn to remain *detached* from the outcome, while believing strongly that the coachee will find their own answers at the pace which suits their development - and not at a pace to suit the coach's impatience!

Rapport, trust and professionalism

Rapport between coach and coachee is essential if the coaching is to maximise the potential both of the coachee and of the coaching process. And from this rapport will come trust.

A coachee needs to feel comfortable with the coach, trusting that the coach is listening with empathy, that the coach is experienced and professional, and that the coaching will produce results.

The coach needs to be able to challenge the coachee's thinking at times, stretching the client to move beyond what they have always done, to discover other ways, new paths and alternative options, as well as an improved sense of wellbeing. Challenging works best in a relationship where trust has already been established.

Normally rapport is built up by allowing the client to talk a bit about themselves, by the coach listening intently, showing that they understand what they hear and take it seriously. In addition, coaches need to show by their coaching behaviour and by their processes that they are professionals and that coaching brings results.

Confidentiality

Respecting confidentiality is another of the cornerstones of coaching. If coachees are to work well with the coach, they must know that all conversations are confidential.

In the workplace this can be difficult but it is essential. The client can only optimise their potential if they are absolutely honest with themselves and with their coach. This is only possible with complete confidentiality. Any written records should be kept in a manner that protects anonymity. And if not required to keep them, the coach should destroy these records when the programme ends.

Own Notes

Own Notes

Chapter 6

Key Coaching Skills

The skill of listening

In coaching, it is useful to consider three levels of listening:

- Superficial
- Active
- Deep

Superficial Listening is what we do if we listen while doing other tasks at the same time. Or, when we are listening and thinking about our own experiences, ready to jump in with *"Oh yes I remember the same thing when I ……"*

Active Listening is when we are listening at a more attentive level. The speaker is really holding our attention and, quite naturally, we react with "Really" "Yes, I see" "Oh how awful" or we may ask questions to find out more. In these ways we show the speaker that we are interested and attentive.

Deep Listening is the listening skill we need as coaches. Deep listening is when we are **totally** focused on the speaker and the meaning of what they are saying. We listen both to what is said and what is unsaid. In our total focus on the client, we are not anxious to contribute ideas, stories or suggestions of our own. There is no chatter in our heads; we allow space for the client both to speak and think. If they pause, we remain silent or may prompt with *"Did you want to say something more about that?"*

When we want to help a client to dig deeper, we may need to ask a different question. However, sometimes we just need to repeat the same one. Here are some questions to help clients to delve deeper:

- *What specifically did you mean by.......?*
- *Can you give an example?*
- *What exactly do you mean about.....?*
- *I notice you mentioned....how important is that to you?*
- *You seem to be ..... What else do you need to say about that?*

Good coaches listen at a deep level to every answer, expecting that **the coachee** will come up with the best solutions for them. Interestingly, when we listen deeply it is easier to avoid jumping in with **our own** solutions.

The skill of powerful questioning

The coach asks questions to help the client think creatively, to raise awareness and to develop responsibility for change and growth. Closed questions (where the answer is *yes* or *no*) can be useful but open questions in coaching help to tease out more, faster. Here are some questions, arranged to reflect the S-GROW model:

S for Strengths and Successes
1. *What is going well?*
2. *What pleased you most about that?*
3. *What other successes have you had?*

G for Goal
4. *What would you like to go away with at the end of today?*
5. *What is your desired outcome for this conversation (session)?*
6. *How will you know you have reached it?*
7. *How could you rephrase that in positive language?*

R for Reality
8. *What is the current situation / issue /context?*
9. *Who else is involved?*
10. *What have you already put in place?*
11. *What assumptions might you be making here?*
12. *In what way are these valid, true, relevant,?*

O for Options
13. *What could be done to move this forward?*
14. *What possibilities are available?*
15. *If you could choose, what would you do?*
16. *What other possible solutions are there?*
17. *What might go wrong?*
18. *What barriers might there be?*
19. *How could you deal with that if it happened?*

W for Will
20. *What needs to happen now?*
21. *What will you do?*
22. *When will you do it?*
23. *Who else will you involve?*
24. *How can they / I support you?*

To finish a coaching conversation or session, the coach can ask a couple of powerful feedback questions, to learn what real value the interaction has given the client and if changes are necessary. You might use these:

To make these sessions as useful as possible for you, would you answer a couple of questions?

1. *What was most useful for you in the session today?*
   or *What did you learn from today's session?*

2. *Is there anything we could do differently next time to make it more effective and useful for you?*

The skill of challenging
Coaching is supportive but it is not cosy. It is unlike a conversation between friends because it is the coach's job to NOT buy in to the coachee's interpretation of events; rather, the coach's function is to help the coachee see the facts clearly and consider alternative interpretations: this can be the stepping stone towards creating better solutions and alternative ways forward.

Therefore, the coach sometimes has to challenge the client and their thinking. Clients differ in how much challenge they want and coaches need to check that the level of challenge is enough and not too much for each individual coachee.

The extent of challenge depends on the tone of voice used: a very direct tone can sound more challenging than a softer one with a lift at the end. It can also be mitigated by the addition of 'softener words' such as *do you think, might, possibly,* as you can see in this example:

When will you do that? (direct words)
When do you think you might do that? (softened)

Challenging questions might be:

- *When will you do that?*
- *What stops you doing that now?*
- *How might that stop you?*
- *Who could improve on that idea?*
- *How might you be encouraging that behaviour?*
- *I notice that you agreed to actions last week which you didn't carry through. What do you think might be the reason?*
- *What else might have had an influence?*

The skill of reflecting back

A coach reflects back information to the coachee for two main reasons. The first is to let the coachee know what has been understood. This guards against the coach making assumptions about meaning. For instance, by saying:

It sounds as if you are angry

the coach avoids **assuming** the coachee is angry and, by reflecting back what was understood, allows the coachee to clarify.

In normal conversation we make many assumptions as a matter of course: we draw inferences and assume we catch the correct meaning. This functions as a way of bonding, of saving time and it creates shared meanings. But coaching is not meant to be a normal conversation! Its purpose is different - not merely to share information and create a bond but to develop awareness, creative thinking and optimised potential.

The second reason is to let the client hear what they have communicated. Very often a client will respond *"Oh I didn't mean that. I meant ...."*. In hearing their own words repeated back, the client realised they had meant something different. Improved clarity in thinking and speaking, and a heightened awareness of these, is part of the benefit to the client of the coaching conversations.

These are some phrases used for reflecting back:

- *I notice that you say......*
- *It sounds as if you feel......*
- *It sounds as if you think .....*
- *It seems that ......*
- *I get the feeling that ......*
- *The impression I'm getting is that you think ....*

The skills of checking back and summarising
Checking and clarifying is often indistinguishable from reflecting back but the aims will be different: to check correct understanding rather than to let the client hear what they have said. In checking, the coach might add *is that correct* to the end:

- *So you feel ...... Have I understood correctly?*
- *You understood ...... Is that correct?*

Summarising is useful at intervals in the coaching conversation. It helps clarify what has been covered and helps the coach and coachee to keep track of the content of the conversation. In addition, it helps the coach to manage the time available. Often starting with *So* (or more obviously *To summarise then*), the coach may use phrases like these:

- *So you feel that* ....
- *So we've covered two reasons for delay. Are there others?*
- *So we've covered the background now. Is that how you see it? Shall we move on to the steps you might take?*
- *So, you've described several options. Can you list them for us both?*

Parking issues

Sometimes a topic will come up in a coaching conversation which, while appearing important, would distract from the topic or goal in hand. In this case, the coach can agree with the client to *park* the new subject. The coach then needs to bring the parked topic into a future session and ask what the client wants to do about it. The coach's skill is in keeping focus, while ensuring that other important subjects are not ignored.

Focus on results

Coaching is a powerful developmental process designed to produce results – but it is not for everyone. And if it is not producing results, it should stop. The good coach monitors progress at every session with the client and checks whether changes to the process are necessary. Keeping a steady focus on results, on reaching goals and outcomes, while including all the areas that the client considers relevant and chooses to bring to the coaching sessions, is a key skill for the successful coach.

Own Notes

Own Notes

Chapter 7

Remarkable Progress

In this chapter we look at four ways for the coach to assist the coachee in making noticeable progress: setting goals, agreeing a first step, the SPOT diagram and the ERR coaching model.

It is important to recognise that both coaching and developmental change are processes and while change can happen very quickly it usually happens over time. It can happen quickly, say, when a catalyst question makes 'the penny drop' and radical change happens as a result. However, it normally takes a period of weeks or months to implement and consolidate changes in deep-rooted behaviour, thinking or attitude. Some say three weeks as a minimum, others 90 days; still others say six to twelve months.

Setting goals

The first step to making remarkable progress is to set a specific goal. If it is written down and dated, better still because this means you can look back on it later and see the progress. Consider the opposite: without a stated goal there is no way to measure achievement or progress; it is too easy to change direction, forget where you were when you started and exactly what you were aiming for. *If you don't know where you are going, how can you know when you have got there?*

When the S-GROW model is used in coaching, the coach asks the coachee what they want to go away with (the outcome or Goal) from the session. This allows the coach to structure the session, manage the timing and the pace so that the goal is reached.

Often there is an overall goal for a coaching programme, to be less retiring in meetings, say, as in the example below.

Although progress would be made in the first session, the aim of coaching is to optimise potential and ensure that the client changes behaviour, creates new habits and gains confidence at a deep level, so the coach should recommend a few sessions. Six sessions is a common choice so that the process, stretched over 2-3 months, gives time for new habits to be firmly established and real development to occur.

The most important aspect of a goal is that it inspires its owner. Make sure that your client *owns* the goal, choosing goals that they really want, not ones that they feel they *should* choose.

Goals should be SMART, couched in positive, inspiring language, focused on moving **towards** rather than moving **away from**. This variation on the SMART acronym is helpful for coaching goals:

S　Stretching
M　Measurable (and therefore specific)
A　Achievable
R　Relevant
T　Time-bound

Below, the coach helps Jo, the coachee, to create a SMART goal:

Jo:　　*I want to be less shy and quiet in meetings. I often have things to say but other people are louder and interrupt. Sometimes I end up thinking it's easier to just keep quiet.*

Coach:　*So how would you like to be in meetings?*

Jo:　　*Well, I'd like to feel confident and seem confident. I'd like to think my ideas are as good as others and worth hearing.*

Coach:　*So you'd like to feel and seem confident and think your ideas are worth hearing at meetings with colleagues. Is that right?*

Jo:　　*Yes it is.*

Coach:　*Would that be a stretch for you or quite easy to achieve?*

Jo: *A bit of a stretch actually. In fact quite a stretch!*

Coach: *Inside, does it feel an exciting stretch or a worrying one?*

Jo: *Oh no, not worrying. Exciting. It would be great.*

Coach: *And how will you know when you have got there?*

The session continues: the coach ensures the goal is specific, pinning down how success will be measured and achieved.

These specifics are not fixed for all time - dates and measures can be changed later - but working to a goal is more effective when specific dates and measures are stated at the start.

Ideally, the goal is a stretch for the client because coaching is about releasing potential not about remaining in the original comfort-zone. As individuals vary in how much stretch is exciting and what is too much, good coaches check this with each client for each goal.

The first step

Sometimes the overall goal seems impossible to achieve and there is an impasse. Say the coachee announces *There's nothing we can do. There's no solution.* At this point, thinking of a first step can be helpful in breaking the block:

- *What first step might you take in the right direction?*
- *What might be a tiny step towards improving this?*
- *What first small step could you take right now?*

Thinking of the first step is often a way in, towards finding the answer for a seemingly intractable situation, and to adopting this strategy for other situations.

The 'first step' approach also helps near the end of a session, when the client wants an action plan but little time is left:

- *What could be your first step?*
- *When could you make time to think through options for Step 2 and email them to me?*

The SPOT Diagram

Strengths	Points to develop
Opportunities	**Threats**

Notes on using the SPOT diagram

The SPOT is derived from the SWOT Analysis tool used in business. It is a useful model for self-analysis or to analyse a job, situation or project; it can help a coachee build confidence and see a situation more clearly. The left-hand column shows the positives and the right the negatives. The top band is internal, the bottom external. *Threats* are any potential barriers or difficulties.

1. The SPOT works well for an overview or to focus on a single area or skill.

2. Have the coachee fill in the 4 boxes. Bullet points are best here as they make it easier to identify the different elements.

3. Completing a personal or job-related SPOT (before, after or during a coaching session) works well to build confidence.

4. The coach may need to prompt with questions, such as:

S
- *What strengths do you have as a manager/leader/etc?*
- *What other plus points do you have?*
- *What might your colleagues add to that list?*
- *What does your boss/deputy/partner appreciate in you?*

P
- *What might colleagues want you to develop or improve?*
- *What further skills will be useful in your career/ with X?*

O
- *How do you see the future developing?*
- *What options are available and what could you create?*

T
- *What could go wrong?*
- *What barriers might there be?*

5. Be sure to deal with Points to Develop and Threats. Use questions like: *How could you deal with that*?

The ERR model

EMOTION

REALITY   RESPONSIBILITY

Notes on using the ERR model

While many new coaches find the S-GROW model answers all their needs, others like to use the ERR model for special circumstances. Because of its high visual impact, it can be an easy one for visual learners to remember.

The ERR works well when the client arrives at the meeting in a state of high emotion or stress. Using this model, the coach asks a question inviting the coachee to express what they are feeling or experiencing, and listens intently to what follows. When a natural pause occurs or when the coachee is ready to move forward, the coach may ask:

- *What would you like to go away with at the end of this session?*
- *How would you like to feel at the end of today's meeting?*
- *What would be for you the most effective way to use the time today?*
- *What would you like to focus on with me today?*

The answer can be surprising – so the coach should not assume the client will want to spend the session on the topic they have just spoken about with such passion.

Moving on to the Reality, the coach can ask questions which encourage the client to focus on facts (this coincides with the R in the S-GROW model). The coach awakens Responsibility by working through options and actions (as in S-GROW), or asks questions such as:

- *Who is responsible here?*
- *What responsibility could you take?*
- *What could be done differently?*
- *What are you assuming (in saying that)?*

Own Notes

Own Notes

Chapter 8

Celebration

The good coach makes time to celebrate success and achievement in all coaching conversations. This does not mean champagne at every turn and is not just about achieving the big goals. Of course these big goals are important but coaching also takes the time to acknowledge little successes as well, those small incremental steps in the right direction. Many professionals do not take time to fully acknowledge their achievements, partly because others quickly create more demands and needs to fill, and partly because they themselves set their sights on the next task.

Celebration might seem like a waste of time but it gives renewed momentum to the client, spurring them on to further successes.

Ackowledging progress

Progress is as much about learning and awareness as about developing new habits and behaviours. To celebrate progress the coachee first needs to notice and acknowledge it!

One way to do this is by the coach asking S-Questions in the coaching conversation. Look back to Chapter 2 for a list of these to use at the start. You may like to add these additional S-Questions:

- *What 'wins' have you had this week?*
- *Which new behaviours have become habits?*
- *What have you learned from doing that?*
- *I've noticed that you seem X these days. What do you think that stems from?*

Another way is to use the SPOT or Wheel. The SPOT diagram can be completed afresh and then compared with the previous version to show up and emphasise achievements. A Wheel can be referred back to, adding new markers with a new date, again to show progress and development.

The Action Sheet is an alternative way to give visual evidence of success and works especially well with clients who are spurred on by achievement.

Visualising success
Visualising, and planning the celebration when success is achieved, can also help individuals in the goal-setting phase.

The Goal Record Sheet overleaf gives several prompts to help the client visualise success and the context for celebration. The coach may need to encourage the client here because the detail will help greatly in making the goal more compelling.

Celebrating success
When a client is reluctant to acknowledge or celebrate successes, or wants to rush on, the coach may wish to ask these questions:

- *How does it feel to see on paper the progress you've made?*
- *What benefits did you expect to experience when you set the goal?*
- *What else have you experienced – which you didn't expect?*
- *How does it feel to savour your success in this way?*
- *What could you learn from that?*
- *I notice some reluctance to acknowledge your achievement. What might be behind that?*
- *How do you plan to celebrate your achievement?*
- *Who could you share this with?*
- *How will you reward yourself?*

Action Plan

Name: .... Date: ....

ACTION STEP	DATE COMPLETED
1.	
2.	
3.	
4.	
5.	
6.	
7.	
8.	
9.	
10.	
11.	
12.	
13.	
14.	
15.	
16.	
17.	
18.	
19.	
20.	
21.	
22.	
23.	
24.	
25.	
26.	
27.	
28.	
29.	
30.	

Today's date: ....

Goal Record Sheet

My goal *worded in positive, inspiring language:*

Date I will achieve it:

How I will celebrate my success:

What will success look like? *Using vivid language, write what you are doing, seeing, enjoying when you have reached your goal. What are people saying?*

Where am I now? *what is the current reality: write a factual description without judgment or analysis*

What actions will I take, with dates?

My supporters / support system:

Affirmations: *use only positive language, without any negatives (eg not, never) describing your goal as if you have already achieved it.*

Notes on using The Goal Record Sheet

Celebrating success is made easier by having a record of the original goal! This can be done on a Goal Record Sheet which also acts as a motivator to the client during the process of achieving the aim. Note that Affirmations are described fully in Chapter 9.

1. Word the goal with present tense *now* verbs: *I can.. I am doing.. I have*

2. Use only positive words, avoiding all negative words like *never, not, no more, not any more*

3. Focus on the positive aspects of the objective so re-phrase as the examples illustrate:

   from: *I am eating less*
   to: *I am choosing to enjoy moderate portions of colourful, appetising, healthy food*

   from: *Negotiations with X are not so lengthy*
   to: *I am easily reaching win-win agreements with X*

Reminders

- Ensure the client dates the sheet
- Consider the support sections. The benefit is in the coachee discovering "allies" and support mechanisms in advance
- The coach may need to prompt with questions such as:
  What is the situation at the moment? (Reality)
  What options are open to you? (Options)
  How can you improve the situation? (Options)
  What will you do as a first step? (Will)

Own Notes

Own Notes

Chapter 9

Limiting Language

When we change our language, we change our thinking. Just try this simple experiment. Say these pairs of sentences to yourself one at a time. Pause after each sentence in the pair, to compare how your thoughts change after saying each.

Pair A
1. *My colleague never meets deadlines. He's hopeless.*
2. *My colleague sometimes meets deadlines.*

Pair B
1. *I'm a great fat lump.*
2. *I weigh more than I'd like.*

In the second sentence of each pair, we can feel a sense of potential, whereas in the first there is a sense of hopelessness. Yet both sentences can apply to the same situation and both can be equally accurate. It is the half-full, half-empty syndrome.

Watch out for limiting language. Usually it either leads to limiting and negative thoughts or it stems from them. Positive statements tend to cheer us up, negative ones to depress us and limit our options. Positive ones build confidence and create options; negative ones sap self-esteem.

As coaches we need to be very aware of the language we use, in order to act as good models for our clients and so that they learn to notice and reduce their own use of limiting language.

So in wording a goal, the coachee learns to avoid using negatives, so that *I'm not smoking any more* might become: *I enjoy feeling fitter each day.*

Half-full or half-empty?

When you hear your coachee describing themselves or a situation in negative terms, draw their attention to it. Help them see that using positive language creates useful options. Ask them to change the words to say the same thing using positive language, then find out from them which version sounds better to them and which is likely to result in more success.

For example, if asked to rephrase: *I'm no good at detail,* the client might produce one of these:

> *I'm good at the big picture.*
> *I choose to let others deal with detail.*
> *I could improve my skills with detail.*
> *When I understand the detail I feel calm.*

Positive self-talk

For many of us, our inner voice is one that criticises, pushes us to do better, comments on what we have done wrong.

> *Why didn't I say something then?*
> *Why couldn't I remember?*
> *I must eat less next time.*
> *I've done nowhere near what I planned.*
> *I've hardly got anything to show for all that time.*
> *I'm so slow at ….*
> *Late again!*

Maybe we have all been taught to strive for perfection. Maybe our bosses, teachers and parents always pointed out what we could do better. Whatever the past, research shows that individuals do better when they feel they are succeeding and loved, so a praise culture would be helpful at work! A word of warning: the praise must be sincere. Just as with the half-full glass, it is a question of finding something positive - and true - in the situation.

The first place to start is in our own heads: using positive *self-talk* to counteract any negative comments that we make and hear.

A warning note: the idea is not to make everything a false rosy colour but to acknowledge what the truth is. Acknowledging strengths does not mean that we encourage the client to think they do everything well. But the client who can separate, and acknowedge fairly, what they do well from what they need to improve, will be in a better frame of mind to work on the necessary improvements than the individual who muddles everything together in a generalised not-good-enough or nothing-needs-changing attitude.

Affirmations

An affirmation is positive self-talk, usually in a single sentence; a set of affirmations would be a number of these. Affirmations can be used to describe and confirm a current strength and achievement, or to describe a goal state as if it is already a reality. Once the affirmation is created, it must be repeated several times every day to have an effect.

Describing a goal state as if it is a reality works for some people. It is like planting a seed in the brain, which then looks for evidence and reminds you to move towards making it true. The coach can guide the coachee to use positive self-talk in this way, as a method of changing habits and attitudes.

Alternatively, the client can use affirmations which *affirm* what is true or starting to happen. For instance:

- *Every day my confidence is growing*
- *My colleagues in Paris easily understand my French*
- *Day by day I'm becoming more punctual*
- *I always look professional and prepare my work well.*

The guidelines for wording affirmations are the same as for wording goals:

1. Only use positive words: avoid *not, never, rarely, not any, nothing*

2. Speak as if it is happening now, so use the present tense: eg *I am running.., I run* (not *I want to*; not *I will run*)

3. Make it a sentence that is easy to say and that inspires you.

4. Say the sentence regularly. At least make sure to say it at night before switching off the light and first thing on waking up as these are times when you are especially receptive.

The more the positive self-talk is practised, the more useful it is and the more encouraged the coachee is to continue the change programme they have started. In fact, it is a mental keep-fit programme, so best done every day!

Keeping fit mentally

These are habits for life for your client: noticing and limiting negative talk and negative beliefs; practising positive self-talk; deciding what to aim for, writing it down, repeating it often and daily.

Like physical keep-fit, it does not work if clients do not keep it going. That is one of the functions of the regular coaching session: the coach re-models the 'healthy' language and 'healthy' thinking habits until they become second nature for the client and they can go it alone.

Avoiding 'try'

Coaches help their clients to avoid using the word *try* in wording goals because it suggests they might fail. Compare these two goals:

I'll try to keep my temper for the next 7 days.
I'll keep my temper for the next 7 days.

You will notice that when *try* is omitted the goal sounds like a commitment: the speaker has promised to keep their temper. In contrast, with *try* included, the speaker is already suggesting that they might not succeed.

Scaling from 0-10

By asking a *scaling* question, the coach can help the coachee to be both more specific and more aware of vague or avoidance language. For instance, when a coachee says *It's quite difficult*, the coach can ask:

> *How difficult is it on a scale of 0 to 10, if 0 is extremely easy and 10 the hardest imaginable?*

The answer is revealing both to coachee and coach, allowing the conversation to move on in a relevant direction.

Own Notes

Own Notes

Chapter 10

Documentation, Contracts and Agreements

It is useful to have some documentation for your coaching conversations, for instance a record sheet, a planning document and a contract or agreement between you and the coachee. The contract or agreement clarifies the coaching relationship and gives a professional impression. Also, it adds a serious note to the proceedings: a coaching session is different from other day-to-day interactions, and has a different purpose, so the fact of having an agreement or contract make this clear.

The Coaching Record Sheet
The Coaching Record Sheet reminds the coach between sessions what went on in the last conversation with this client; it is also a reminder to the coach to take time to reflect after each session.

The Individual Planner Sheet
The rationale behind using a planner document is that it gives the coach a focus for discussing a longer term goal with the coachee. The example page shows how the sheet might be filled in.

When the coach goes from one session to the next with the same client but without a planning document, the longer term initial goal may be replaced by fire-fighting on short-term issues or crises which arise for the coachee. This is perfectly acceptable if the coachee seriously chooses to switch focus. However, as the coach, you should remind the coachee of the original goal, prompt them to decide whether it is still relevant and, if it is, keep it in focus so that progress can be made.

The Client's Coaching Preparation Form

Clients like this form because it helps them obtain maximum value from each coaching session. If emailed in advance to the coach, it acts as a useful time-saver in the session too.

The Contract or Agreement

Whether a coaching contract or agreement is appropriate will depend to some extent on whether coaches formally offer coaching sessions to colleagues and others, or whether they only use coaching skills as part of a range of managerial skills.

For the latter situation, when the manager or leader uses coaching among many other skills to lead and develop their teams, a coaching agreement or contract would usually be inadvisable. In this context the word *coaching* may not be used at all. This leader, from the managing director working with a team of directors to the teacher working with a group of students or children, may not wish to overtly 'coach'.

At the other extreme, an organisation, university or school may offer formal coaching sessions for all new managers or, via a booking system, for all colleagues.

Somewhere in the middle, a manager might give a monthly coaching session to each member of their team, alongside using some coaching skills as relevant in other managerial interactions.

For the formal coaching sessions, a coaching agreement or contract sets the conversations apart from other work interactions and gives the coach licence to behave in a clearly different, coach-like way.

The contract may look like the sample included here or be quite different, created to suit the specific work context. To change just a few words on the sample included here, just cross them out and initial the correction with your client.

The Coaching Record Sheet

Client: .... Date of session: ....

Coach: .... Number of this session: ....

Main Points discussed

What's going well ? What are you good at? (S-Factor)

Desired outcome of session (Goal)

Current situation (Reality)

Opportunities available (Options)

What will you do (Will)	**When**	**Scale**

Client feedback *So that I can help you better, what was useful for you today?*

Is there anything you'd like me to change to make it more useful?

Coach's reflections after the session

Individual Planner Sheet

Coachee: .... Coach: .... Date: ....

Coachee's job role:

Current challenges and priorities

Goals

1.

2.

3.

4.

5.

Action	Dates

Resources

Other notes

Coachee signature................................ Coach signature................................

Example

Individual Planner Sheet

Coachee: .... Coach: .... Date: ....

Coachee's job role: *CPD Manager*

Current challenges and priorities

New system for staff appraisal

2 new middle managers

To build the new management team

Improve employee morale

Goals

1. *To review induction system for new managers and include 1:1 coaching*

2. *To learn about different ways of Performance Management and appraisals*

3. *To understand the recent changes in legislation that affect PM*

4. *To study the data from recent employee feedback survey and come up with strategies to discuss at October senior management meeting*

Action	Dates
• *Review current induction*	*by 30 June 08*
• *Discuss coaching addition with my coach*	*July*
• *Book + attend workshop re employee legislation*	*20 June*
• *Talk to X and Y re their PM systems*	*w/b 23 June*
• *Buy + read 'Coaching in Performance Management'*	*by 30 June/1 Sept*

Resources

PM colleagues X and Y + network

My coach

Internet - Amazon

Other notes

Coachee signature................................ Coach signature................................

Client's Coaching Preparation Form

Coachee: .... **Date:** ....

What have I accomplished since our last call? (Your wins)

What did I not get done, but intended to do:

The challenges (a positive word for problems) I now face are:

The opportunities available to me now are:

I want to use my coach during the call to:

What was the most useful aspect of my last coaching conversation and why?

I'd also like to tell you …

© Oxford Professional Consulting 2008

Coaching Agreement

Welcome to the coaching partnership. I look forward to coaching you and would like to explain the procedures we will be following.

Calls/meetings   We meet on time at the agreed time /date / location. Our agreement includes up to 2 hours of coaching per calendar month, face-to-face or by phone as agreed.

Changes   If you need to reschedule, please give me 1 week's notice if possible. In emergency situations, we will work something out. However, coaching works best with 100% commitment on both sides. It does not produce results if momentum is disrupted by cancelled sessions.

Extra Time   You may call or e-mail me between sessions if you need advice, have a problem or want to share a success with me. This is part of the support I offer. I would ask that you keep calls to 5-10 minutes.

Preparation   I ask my clients to complete a Coaching Preparation Form and e-mail it to me 24 hours before each session. This saves time in our session but is optional.

Problems   Please be open and honest with me if you are not getting what you need from our coaching. I am 100% committed to supporting you.

Payment   Fees are in advance for an agreed number of sessions or period. Cheques made payable to .... please. Receipts available.

Requests   I may ask you to take an action between our sessions and you are free to accept or decline. The purpose will always be for your benefit, to make progress and to increase learning.

Confidentiality   All our sessions will be totally confidential.

I confirm that I have read and agree to the above

Signed: .... Client   Date: ....

Signed: .... Coach   Date: ....

© Oxford Professional Consulting 2008

Own Notes

Own Notes

Chapter 11

Coaching in Management

There are many opportunities to benefit from using coaching skills if you have a management role: in appraisals and performance management schemes, leadership development, building and leading teams, developing individuals and in induction programmes for staff in new roles. As well, there is executive coaching for senior leaders and team coaching.

Ideally, the company or organisation will develop all of its leaders, equipping them with the tools, skills and techniques to create and maintain a winning culture – one where coaching is integrated into everyday leadership style rather than being an occasional activity or relegated to the annual appraisal interview only.

The manager as coach
Instead of telling their team what to do and being responsible for finding every solution, managers can use coaching skills to elicit answers from the team and encourage team ownership of processes and results. Many managers will use coaching skills alongside other management skills, interchangeably. Others choose to establish a regular formal coaching session for each member of the team, seeing this as a chance to develop each person in a more sustained way than with just a once-a-year appraisal meeting.

"It gives me the chance to find out more about each member of my team and to support each one in getting where they want to go," said one manager who sees each team member for an hour's coaching session every couple of months. "I think the team is more cohesive as a result and performance has improved."

Development and performance coaching

Coaching is known to be effective in improving performance whether it is the coachee or the manager who instigates the intervention. There are three basic models:

1. Coaching is used alone
2. Coaching and mentoring are used together
3. Group training takes place first, followed by individual coaching to establish new habits and ensure implementation

Coaching alone and coaching with mentoring

Coaching alone, without giving advice, is very powerful in developing potential and encouraging creative thinking from the coachee. However, where the coach has a great deal of expertise in the area on which the coachee is being coached, it is likely that the coach will alternate coaching with mentoring, where mentoring means giving advice. To give no advice at all when they have much useful knowledge would seem perverse. Other managers in this situation may choose to coach first and then, at the end of the meeting, give some ideas in the role of mentor.

Some managers become so used to managing in a coaching way that it effortlessly and unnoticeably becomes their management style.

Others find it useful to explain what they are doing when they use a coaching style, with words such as these at the start of a meeting:

> *I'm going to use some coaching skills (techniques) in running this meeting because that way you, rather than me, will be the key player/s. Rather than me imposing my ideas, I'll be asking you. I'm sure we will both (all) find it useful.*

Training followed by individual coaching

When coaching follows training it enables the individual to examine their own job situation in the light of the new knowledge and skills acquired in the training. They are able to work out the implications and then devise and commit to an action plan of their own for implementing the new skills and ideas. This is recognised as a highly efficient way to improve performance. According to a survey from the Chartered Institute of Personnel Development in 2004, productivity was increased by over 22% through training alone, while it rose by 88% with training and coaching combined.

The S-Factor for meetings and with teams

The S-GROW model is very effective in meetings, also in a team coaching or facilitating context. Again some managers choose to 'frame up' what they are doing at the start, so that individuals are not irritated by unaccustomed questions and what they may see as lack of direction from their leader.

> *I'm going to use some coaching skills and techniques in running this meeting because I believe that they are useful to help us get maximum creativity as a team. If it feels a bit unusual at first, please bear with me. I've found these techniques very useful myself when I've been on the receiving end.*

Others will prefer to use the S-GROW structure for the meeting without making this overt.

It can be useful to facilitate with two coaches present, so that one facilitates and runs the session while the other takes notes, say on a flipchart. Then there are two available when the group divides into smaller working groups, as well as when a range of opinions or information is sought.

Performance Management and appraisal interviews

Performance Management is carried out in many organisations with one annual appraisal meeting, one-to-one, between the employee and their line-manager. Depending on the organisation, there may be a great deal of pre-guidance for one or both parties, or very little. Even where there are good intentions, and good practices already in place, there may be room for a more developmental, appraisee-centred approach; the skills, practice and principles of coaching are very relevant here.

Some of the aims of coaching and appraising are very similar: to acknowledge and celebrate success, to optimise potential by supporting and stretching the individual. A coach also wants to stimulate thinking, be a thinking partner, support and challenge the coachee. For good development work a coach sees the client every week or two weeks over a period of 3 months to a year; in this way momentum is created, responsibility and accountability are increased, feeding achievement and growth.

Following a coaching approach in an appraisal interview could be beneficial in a variety of ways. The meeting could follow the S-GROW model; a SPOT diagram could be used to celebrate first strengths and achievements then consider areas to develop; coaching could be used to work through areas of poor performance or development points. The appraiser could take the role of the thinking partner, supporting and challenging like a coach.

Coaching principles and practices to consider for appraisals are:

1. asking what the colleague wants to go away from the meeting with, rather than assuming you both know
2. spending more time on Strengths through coaching prompts, not only listing wins from the year
3. asking about long-term goals and ambitions before looking at the next year objectives
4. really believing in the coachee and their potential
5. doing a SPOT analysis or S-Wheel with coaching questions

6. getting the coachee to choose objectives which they really want, not that they feel they 'should' choose
7. encouraging them to choose goals that move them beyond the comfort-zone into a stretching zone, avoiding both 'coasting' and negative stress
8. encouraging growth in weak areas and directly challenging complacency
9. setting goals for three months at a time rather than for a year, ensuring more regular progress conversations and thus the opportunity to maintain high performance, morale and momentum
10. structuring the meeting round the S-GROW model, with plenty of emphasis on the S-Factors before moving on to constructive planning of new goals

Just one proviso. For the coaching approach to have a powerful effect in appraisals, the managers appraising need to have attended a thorough training in coaching basics, including a mix of coaching principles, skills and practice. Talking about the skills alone is not enough because it *sounds* very simple. "It's not as easy as it looks" is a common comment from learner coaches trying to hold back from giving advice and to use more open questions.

Own Notes

Own Notes

Chapter 12

Coaching in Education

Coaching was part of the government's plans for education in the National Strategy document of 2004 and it clearly has many potential benefits for education. However, what is practised in schools is often very different from the type of coaching promoted by professional associations in the UK, such as the International Coaching Federation (ICF) and the Association of Coaching (AC), and by this book.

In education, what is often called coaching is what the ICF, the AC and this book would call mentoring. We three (and many other organisations) make a clear distinction between mentoring and coaching, while acknowledging that they both share certain skills and practices. Mentoring is seen as guidance from a senior colleague. It is usually done by a person who is more experienced in the client's growth area and usually includes, or is based on, the mentor's advice. By contrast, coaching does not offer advice because its focus is on the coachee finding their own best solutions. The coach does not need to be an expert in the coachee's field. The coach's aim is to extend the coachee's creative thinking and develop awareness and accountability, with a view to professional development, personal growth and practical results.

Our experience in UK schools, colleges and universities has shown that, while the GROW model is widely acclaimed as a problem-solving tool and coaching is talked about, what goes on in the name of coaching is often mentoring. We have found, too, that once introduced to it, staff very much appreciate coaching, from headteachers through middle managers to newly qualified teachers and lecturers. We have had these comments from teachers:

"It is a relief to be listened to and heard"
"It's wonderful to have the space to think and come up with new solutions"
"Coaching questions help me think differently"
"Ideas and ways forward come more quickly and are better."

From those in a management position we hear the same. The coach's questions give rise to more creative thinking; some solutions come more quickly while others are more innovative, inspiring and beneficial. In addition, coaching often helps the exhausted professional to re-awaken their enthusiasm for the job; through it they learn new ways to deal with the pressures of the Three Ts - tasks, targets and tiredness.

Co-coaching

Co-coaching (peer coaching) is discussed in the National Strategies paper referred to above, as a process whereby two teachers plan a lesson together, watch each other's lesson and then have a conversation about it. The watching teacher may contribute ideas at both the first and third steps; thus, if senior or more experienced, they are likely to mentor or take over rather than coach. We call this peer-mentoring.

Peer-mentoring as a co-operative teaching activity has undoubted value. In addition, as an option to use alongside and to enhance peer-mentoring in schools, we recommend including coaching in the first and third steps.[1]

By including aspects of the coaching approach, the balance is changed and a different 'thinking partnership' is created, resulting in increased confidence, awareness, responsibility

---

1   Our own method is called Co-Coaching PLUS. What it adds are coaching skills and structures in order to extend creative thinking in a different way. In the Co-Coaching PLUS model, if Teacher A does the first lesson, Teacher B uses coaching skills in the pre-lesson conversation and in the post-lesson phase, thus allowing Teacher A to think through their own practice and how to improve it.

and growth of the coachee - and also of the coach. A session of focused training in coaching skills is needed to start, then regular coaching support.

This peer-*coaching*, based on improving the teacher's own self-analysis and thinking processes, complements the peer-*mentoring* which is based on joint planning and sharing of ideas with a partner teacher.

6th-Form Tutors, Learning Mentors and Progression Coaches

The 6th form tutor in secondary school is expected to help 6th formers decide on career options and solve personal problems. Added to that, the tutors want to support 6th formers in maximising their potential. Coaching is a perfect fit with these aims.

Learning Mentors and Progression Coaches are employed in some schools, respectively, to help pupils improve their learning and stay longer in education. Despite their different job-titles, both tend to advise pupils and students. However, they discover great benefits in using coaching instead and as well in these conversations. By using coaching skills, they help the learners to do more thinking themselves. They discover the learner's own solutions are better because they suit *the learner's* real goals and motivation. In addition, the coaching process builds student confidence in being able to find their own answers, being responsible and being held accountable for actions they agree to carry out.

We would never assert that coaching is best in all situations – it is not. Mentor and advisor roles are very valuable in schools, as of course is teaching. However, the full benefits of coaching are only accessed by schools and colleges where it is fully understood to be distinct from mentoring.

In our experience, the reactions of 6th-form tutors, Progression Coaches and Learning Mentors to coaching are very similar: within minutes they see the potential for coaching skills to magnify the benefits they can give to students and they are keen to learn and practise them. Initially there is some difficulty in abandoning the ingrained habit of offering ideas, sometimes a real shower of suggestions, before the learner has a chance to provide their own. But quickly the distinct skills of coaching are understood and real benefits experienced, even during the practice exercises.

They are not coaches after this quick introductory training; however, they have learnt some key coaching skills and principles which they can apply, as appropriate, in their mentor roles to add greater value than before.

Coaching skills for 6th-formers

In some schools, the students themselves have been taught coaching skills. As in other contexts described above, this can be done in an overt or indirect way. To give two examples: in one case the older students and 6th-formers have attended a specific course to train them to coach other pupils in the school. In another case, a teacher talks of "coaching time out" and prompts his primary school class to consider questions like these:

What is going on?
What kind of a classroom / behaviour / result do we want?
What will we feel like when it's like that?
What is happening now? What are we doing now?
What could we do instead?
What shall we agree to do? Who will do it?
How can we help each other to be sure to do that?
When do we agree to carry out our actions?

Just as schools have found that bullying can be dealt with by trained pupil counsellors, they may find that coaching is a service pupils can be trained to provide for each other.

Own Notes

Own Notes

Chapter 13

Continuing Professional Development for Coaches in the Workplace

It may be time for you to take a recognised coaching qualification. Or you may have one already and be using coaching skills at work. Maybe you are considering a second, more advanced qualification. For anyone serious about coaching in the workplace or wanting to become a professional coach, and without a recognised qualification, we recommend a course leading to coaching qualifications from the Institute of Leadership and Management (ILM).

The ILM qualifications are very practical awards for workplace coaches, whether starting out as managers (Level 3) or more experienced managers and leaders (Level 5 and above). Each course involves input, interaction and frequent practice exercises with feedback and real coaching tasks. As with most qualifications, there is no doubt that doing both courses (Level 3 and Level 5) gives candidates an even better grounding and deeper knowledge of the subject than just one course.[1]

Gaining a qualification will not only teach you more about coaching and improve your skills; it is likely to make you an enthusiastic champion for coaching. You may become a prime mover in creating and supporting a winning culture in your organisation - a culture where there is enthusiasm, inspiration and high quality results, where coaching is

---

1   Details of Oxford Professional Consulting courses leading to ILM coaching qualifications can be obtained from the address on page 148.

integrated into management and leadership style and is not just an occasional activity.

Professional coaching associations

The International Coaching Federation (ICF) and the Coaching Association (CA) are two key professional associations in the UK to consider joining, if you are serious about coaching well. These organisations strongly advocate that a responsible coach should continuously be developing their skills. They therefore offer continuing professional development for all their members, through tele-classes and longer programmes.

Both the ICF and CA operate a programme of 1-day and evening events, to which they normally welcome both members and non-members. There are also tele-seminars to attend by telephone.

Coaching networks

Find out about coaching networks in your area. Some meet for a couple of hours every month while others offer a regular coaching development day every 3 months or so.

An example of the latter is the Newcastle Coaching Network which draws schools together for Continuous Professional Development (CPD) in coaching. It holds a Coaching CPD Day every school term throughout the academic year, for those using coaching in the education sector. The aim of the Coaching CPD Days is to ensure high quality in coaching in schools, colleges and universities across the Local Authority. Without this regular input, the principles and practices of quality coaching - and the enthusiasm for it - may be diluted, due to the many other pressures and priorities in schools today.

The Coaching CPD Days are attended by those interested in or already using coaching in schools or colleges in Newcastle upon Tyne, some already qualified as workplace coaches and others very inexperienced. They invite an experienced coach to present and run the workshop, including a range of activities to develop coaching skills. Speakers on specialist topics and coaching case-studies update the participants and facilitate the sharing of good practice.

Additionally, it is worth joining a coaches' support group of which there are many informal ones in UK towns and cities. You may find that these are often attended by free-lance life-coaches, for whom it replaces the workplace colleagues that they may not have. For the workplace coach, these groups are useful because life-coaches and workplace coaches share similar coaching models, methods and ethics and can learn from each other's experiences.

Many of these informal groups meet regularly and some arrange their own visiting speakers to give workshops at reduced prices. This is an inexpensive way to extend your coaching skills, while deepening your understanding of coaching and widening your network of colleagues.

The Coaching Academy
Based in London, the Coaching Academy has a wide range of high-quality 1-day workshops as well as longer diploma courses. The training takes place at weekends in a venue near London. Experienced and specialist coaching trainers cover topics from Youth Coaching to Executive Coaching and how to market your coaching business. The Academy also operates a free taster course which is worth attending for added experience.

Coaching literature
There is a wide range of coaching books on the market and some good coaching magazines are available. At the end of this chapter are some titles for a range of reading tastes.

Hiring your own coach

A good way to learn more about coaching is to hire your own coach to work with you to optimise your own professional performance. You are coached to move ahead on topics you choose while at the same time you learn how a professional coach runs a session, starts a coaching programme and what exercises they use. You also learn what it feels like to be at the receiving end of a one-to-one development process which increases awareness, accountability and personal learning.

Most coaches will offer a programme of 6 sessions which you can spread over a 3-month period. It is a very worthwhile investment.

Some recommended books on coaching

Coaching for Performance by John Whitmore
Time to Think by Nancy Kline
Coaching with NLP by Joseph O'Connor and Andrea Lages
Executive Coaching with Backbone and Heart by Mary Beth O'Neill
Coaching in Schools by Judith Tolhurst
Coaching Solutions by Will Thomas and Alistair Smith
The Evolution of Peer Coaching by Beverly Showers & Bruce Joyce

Coaching magazines recommended

Coaching at Work magazine from the CIPD
Personal Success magazine from The Coaching Academy

Interesting websites related to coaching

www.internationalcoachingfederation.com
www.coachingnetwork.org.uk
www.oxfordprofessionalcoaching.com
www.hanoverfoundation.org.uk
www.emccouncil.org.uk
www.cipd.co.uk/coachingatwork/presales.htm?redir=unsubs
www.the-coaching-academy.com

Own Notes

Own Notes

Chapter 14

Three Favourites

Getting Present

Before a coaching or training session it is essential for the coach to be fully in the present, having left any issues or personal and work concerns behind. So it is vital to plan some time in the diary before coaching to prepare the mind. However, as even the best-laid plans can go awry, the following exercise can be done along with the client if necessary. It can be done in 2-3 minutes, or you can take longer. You can do it for your client just because it seems a good idea or if they arrive in need of a 'clearing' exercise.

When reading the instructions aloud, speak with a calm, measured pace and relaxing tone, pausing gently after each point.

Instructions:

- *Take a few deep breaths, sit back in your chair with both feet on the ground and close your eyes.*
- *Feel the chair against your back, the floor under your feet.*
- *Let chatter and intrusive thoughts float out of your head; just relax for a few moments…..*
- *Decide what you will leave behind as you go into this session…*
- *Let go of all thoughts of rush .. work .. things you have to do…*
  ………….
- *Now, think about what you want to bring to this session. (It might be curiosity, an open mind; it might be ambition and energy.)…………..*
- *Pause, and open your eyes when you are ready.*

Above the Line

This idea is most often used for group coaching but could be adapted for a one-to-one situation. Look at the picture on the next page to see 'the line'. Each individual chooses whether to stay 'above the line' or 'below the line' and the picture makes it very obvious which is more enjoyable and productive!

Instructions:

Show the chart or draw your own on a flip-chart, explaining how it works and illustrating on your flip. If you are reading the words below, be sure to pause at relevant places as you explain the diagram.

1. *This is The Line* (show the line).
2. *You choose to stay Above the Line* (show) *or Below it* (show).
3. *When you are above the line you are responsible, accountable, solution-focused. You feel excited, enthusiastic. It's fun!*
4. *When you choose to be Below the Line you use excuses, blame, explanations. You focus on problems and barriers. You soon feel stuck and depressed.*
5. *Who commits to staying above the line for the session (or day, week or period)?*

Usually everyone then raises their hand. You have a conversation with the one who does not: they usually change their mind or they may decide the session is not for them and leave.

I learnt this from my own coach. I find it a very useful introduction before a team coaching session or meeting. We find it is important to use it every time, because that way you get commitment and accountability from every person in the group for each session.

Above the Line

IDEAS   **Responsible**

ENERGY   **Accountable**

FUN   **Solutions**

Blame

DEPRESSED   **Excuses**

STUCK   **Explanations**

Problems

Below the Line

Fact & Fiction Exercise

This exercise helps to reduce an issue to manageable size. It is particularly useful when the client is very worried about something or you need to build confidence, because it helps obtain a 'sense of proportion'.

The exercise is also good for working with limiting beliefs. The instructions below are self-explanatory but there is also an example to look at on the next page. The exercise can be given to the client as a homework task or done in the session.

Once they are familiar with this exercise, some clients like to rename the Fiction column, for example as Interpretations or Assumptions, even Drama, or Soap Opera.

Instructions:

1.   *List in the Fiction column any issues, problems or challenges you are finding difficult to deal with. Write just a few words per item.*

2.   *Opposite each item in the Fiction column, list all Facts you know about that item. Exclude opinions and feelings, only include provable facts.*

3.   *Fiction is just a label. Choose to see the Fiction items as **interpretations** not the truth.*

4.   *Bring your paper to your coaching session to discuss with your coach, even if you have not completed the exercise.*

Fact & Fiction

FACT	FICTION

Acknowledgements to the Landmark Foundation for the fact-fiction terminology

Fact & Fiction: example

Client: *Work is terrible. My line-manager has decided to change the way we work and it's a complete mess.*

FACT	FICTION
• I don't know if the new plan will work or not. • The new plan is different from what we were doing. • Sometimes he and I work well together. We worked well on X and Y. • He listened to what I said about A. • His decision may be good for us. • I have no concrete evidence that he doesn't care what we think.	• It'll never work. • He doesn't believe I can do the job. • We don't get on and he doesn't respect me. • I can't get through to him. • He's made the wrong decision and doesn't care what we think.

Own Notes

Own Notes

Chapter 15

Your Own Records

In this chapter are the following worksheets and checklists, specifically for you to keep your own records:

Coaching Ideas to Try

Evaluating My Own Coaching – checklist

Coaching Hours So Far

Coaching CPD and Notes - planned and achieved

Coaching Ideas to Try

New ideas to try

....

....

....

....

....

....

....

Details to check

....

....

....

....

....

....

....

Useful pages to use when coaching

....

....

....

....

....

....

....

Evaluating My Coaching Skills
Checklist

Date: ....

What 3 benefits did the client receive from the session?

What 3 things did I do well in this session?

How well did I listen?

How far was I non-judgemental, believing 100% in the coachee's potential?

How well did I reframe and reflect back?

How well did I check rather than assuming I understood?

How far did I use open questions?

How well did I manage the time?

Did I obtain commitment to action within a time frame? How far did that suit the coachee's preferred outcome for the session?

How can I improve my coaching skills next time?

Coaching Hours: Record

Coaching Hours	Date
....	....
....	....
....	....
....	....
....	....
....	....
....	....
....	....
....	....
....	....
....	....
....	....
....	....
....	....
....	....
....	....
....	....
....	....
....	....
....	....
....	....

CPD Records and Notes

Coaching qualifications and courses	Date completed
....	....
....	....
....	....
....	....
....	....
....	....
....	....
....	....
....	....
....	....
....	....
....	....
....	....
....	....
....	....
....	....
....	....
....	....
....	....
....	....

Coaching CPD can include being coached yourself, coaching books, magazines, courses, discussion forums, coaching clubs and networks, websites and e-courses.

Useful Contacts and Phone Numbers

Contact Name	Email/Telephone
....	....
....	....
....	....
....	....
....	....
....	....
....	....
....	....
....	....
....	....
....	....
....	....
....	....
....	....
....	....
....	....
....	....
....	....
....	....
....	....

Own Notes

Own Notes

Own Notes

Coaching Services
from Oxford Professional Consulting

For companies and organisations

Individual Coaching Programmes for leadership, development, performance (as a stand-alone package or to implement learning after a training course)
Basic Coaching Programme
Advanced Coaching Programme
Laser Coaching (half-day or full-day)

Taster Programmes for groups
Leadership Coaching Taster
Powerful Processes to Improve Results

Skills Development for groups or an individual
Presentation Coaching
Diction Coaching
Writing Coaching
Intercultural Skills Coaching

Coaching Skills Workshops
For Business
Coaching Skills for the Workplace
Intercultural Coaching Skills for Managers

For Education
Introduction to Coaching Skills
Co-Coaching PLUS for Schools
Coaching Inset for Schools

For Business and Education
Courses leading to ILM awards in workplace coaching at Levels 3 and 5

Coaching Workshops
The 7 Steps to Understanding Executive Coaching
The 7 Steps to Understanding Coaching in Education

FREE Workshop – ask for details

Other Workshops
Hi-Impact Quarterly Planning Day
Training, facilitating and consulting services for leaders and teams, in the UK and internationally

Contact Oxford Professional Consulting for details or a consultation at info@oxfordprofessionalconsulting.com or on tel: (UK) 01865 436 791 (international) +44 1865 436 791

What people say about Alison Haill's coaching, the coaching skills workshops she runs and coaching in general.

"Alison's no-nonsense approach to having me get results is the main reason that my business has moved on so strongly and so quickly. I have no hesitation in commending her to anyone seeking similar results. Without coaching I would not have bothered to apply myself over and over to getting the result that I wanted. Through coaching I saw that I was failing to value all the expertise I had, and I determined to approach my new career as an expert. This made a huge difference, and freed me to start creating powerful relationships with a new team and to be bold and self expressed with my clients."

Managing Director, UK

"She went straight to the point without wasting time talking about irrelevant things and I liked her efficient approach. At the same time she had a friendly manner towards me and the subjects I raised, so I quickly felt very much at ease. Follow-up questions were from time to time rather surprising but all the same gave me very relevant and useful insights. I found the external viewpoint and her approach to my issues very valuable in helping me work out my way forward."

HR manager, Norway

"Alison recognised where I was and pushed me to articulate what I felt, (asking) questions to make me find my own solutions. Working very precisely. The meticulous way we worked helped me. The questions and dialogue encouraged me to sustain the approach that I'd worked out through day-to-day and long-term prospects. (I've gained) masses of things (as a result of coaching): detachment; a fairer self-assessment of myself, strengths as well as weaknesses; insight into how my boss communicates and how I do, helping me to deal with it; my own professionalism and worth as a free standing professional...."

Senior manager, UK

"I thought the course was exceptional. I thought the style and delivery were both excellent. I felt at ease at once and able to ask questions. I also felt the trainers were extremely knowledgeable on the area."

Teacher, UK

"This really was a peach of a course for simply explaining in a logical and understated way the coaching and mentoring foundations. Alison quickly dispelled my incorrect notions, giving us ample opportunities to put tools and techniques into practice for fast effect, in my case to further help my clients work creatively with us to significantly improve their results... A thought-provoking day more so than the more common high power ra-ra types."

Managing Director, UK

"(In the *Hi-Impact Quarterly Planning Day*) I got an excellent opportunity for reflection and for planning the activities of my business for the next 3 months."

Managing Director, Italy

"I see coaching as a crucial tool for personal and professional development and for working with individuals. It develops leadership at all levels – tapping into (the) individual potential of each member of your team. The fact you've got more motivated staff with better developed skills means the knock-on effect is in quality and emotional engagement, and in better results"

Senior manager, UK

"The only way to drive up standards is to get staff working creatively and effectively all the time. Coaching can help us do this."

Headteacher, UK